PLANT PARTS

Why Do Plants Have Roots?

Celeste Bishop

PowerKiDS press.

New York

Published in 2016 by The Rosen Publishing Group, Inc.
29 East 21st Street, New York, NY 10010

First Edition

Editor: Sarah Machajewski
Book Design: Mickey Harmon

Photo Credits: Cover, p. 6 (plant) Filipe B. Varela/Shutterstock.com; cover (sky) Elenamiv/Shutterstock.com; cover, p. 1 (logo, frame) Perfect Vectors/Shutterstock.com; cover, pp. 1, 3–4, 7–8, 11–12, 15–16, 19–20, 23–24 (background) djgis/Shutterstock.com; p. 5 Richard Griffin/Shutterstock.com; p. 9 Brian A Jackson/Shutterstock.com; p. 10 LilKar/Shutterstock.com; p. 13 Gyuszko-Photo/Shutterstock.com; p. 14 Yuji Sakai/Photodisc/Getty Images; pp. 17, 18 showcake/Shutterstock.com; p. 21 Sergiy Bykhunenko/Shutterstock.com; p. 22 Julie Campbell/Shutterstock.com

Library of Congress Cataloging-in-Publication Data

Bishop, Celeste, author.
 Why do plants have roots? / Celeste Bishop.
    pages cm. — (Plant parts)
 Includes index.
 ISBN 978-1-5081-4225-6 (pbk.)
 ISBN 978-1-5081-4226-3 (6 pack)
 ISBN 978-1-5081-4227-0 (library binding)
 1. Roots (Botany)—Juvenile literature. 2. Plants—Juvenile literature. I. Title.
 QK644.B564 2016
 575.5'4—dc23
                            2015021402

Manufactured in the United States of America

CPSIA Compliance Information: Batch #BW16PK: For Further Information contact Rosen Publishing, New York, New York at 1-800-237-9932

Contents

You can't always see every part of a plant. Roots are almost always hidden!

5

Roots grow under the ground. They have many important jobs.

Roots keep a plant in the ground. It won't blow away or tip over.

Roots help a plant stand up straight.

Roots take in water from the dirt.
Plants need water to grow.

Roots also take in nutrients. Nutrients are tiny pieces of matter. Plants need them to grow, too.

There are two kinds of roots.
A **taproot** is long and thick.
It points down.

Fibrous roots have many small roots. They grow throughout the dirt.

Many plants have roots we can eat. Did you know carrots and beets are roots?

The next time you go outside, look at the ground. Are there roots under there?

Words to Know

fibrous root

taproot

Index

F
fibrous roots, 19

N
nutrients, 15

T
taproot, 16

W
water, 12

Websites

Due to the changing nature of Internet links, PowerKids Press has developed an online list of websites related to the subject of this book. This site is updated regularly. Please use this link to access the list: www.powerkidslinks.com/part/root